ικφλφδλδακκακκκακκακκκ,μ

The EYE's
of JUNE

κκλδλκαιρϖ,νν

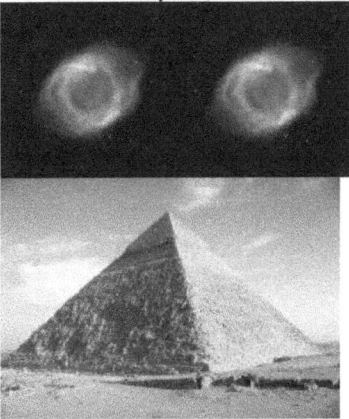

Written by: David Morgan Jr.

Published by: Big Break Entertainment

While the author have made every effort to provide accurate
telephone numbers and Internet addresses at the time of
publication, neither the publisher nor the author assume any
responsibility for errors, or for change that occur after
publication.

First Big Break Entertainment trade paperback edition:
October 08, 2008
Big Break Entertainment trade paperback ISBN:
        978-0-615-25533-0

Printed in the United States of America.

This book is Dedicated to the one's
who never doubted me, Cleavotta,
Destiney, and Dae'Jon and if they did at
least they kept it to themselves.

Wow! Who would ever think that someone would be reading my story? It's strange because I wasn't always a bestselling author. I didn't always have my own Entertainment Company. In fact there was a time when I didn't have any money at all. Times when me and my family were homeless with no where to stay, steps away from a homeless shelter. I know some of ya'll know exactly what I mean, but in the pages of this book I'm going to tell you how I became financially independent. It wasn't through the homelessness I endured, or the lack of family and friend support, nor the illegal living I once involved myself in for survival. (I have never done anything illegal since the birth of my kids).

There where times when I made over $2000 dollars a day, and that did not get me to financial freedom. It was like I knew how to make money, but yet I did not know what to do with it once I made it. The reason I figured this out was because soon after I made the money, I would be broke. I didn't truly become wealthy until I truly understood what money was and how it circulated.

95% of he world know what money is. They know that money is used to buy the things that you want and don't have. 85% of the world know how to make money whether legal or illegal. The sad thing is that only about 35% of the world knows how powerful money is. And until you understand what money is and what its purpose is, can you become financially independent.

My main concern is not how you make your money. It's what you do

with your money that concerns me.
The funny thing about it is that the
one's who make money illegally has a
chance to become financially free faster
due to the fact that their the one's with
the money to back their decisions.
Most people with the best ideals have
no money and no sense of hustle. The
one's that make the most money really
have no business sense at all, because if
they did they would quit that high
paying job or stop doing whatever it is
they are doing illegal. I stopped doing
illegal things due to the fact that I got
tried of going to jail and prison. After
awhile your family and friends get tried
of putting money on your books, or
sending you a package. (God forbid).

It's hard for poor people to become
wealthy because they don't teach us
about money in school or at home.
Most people don't have wealthy friends

to set good examples. School is only intended to prepare us to get a job. School teaches us how to work. School doesn't teach us how to create those businesses that puts others to work. If you are in school your teacher's are going to teach you the same thing as everyone else in some form or fashion.

English, math, science, health, physical education, and history, and with that education you become Teachers, doctors, lawyers, scientist, coaches, ect. We become products of society. Now there is nothing wrong with becoming those things because the world needs doctors, lawyers, cooks, and police officers to keep the world revolving. Now what about the one's who get bad grades or drop out of school? Society teaches us that people who drop out of school are least likely to make it in the real world. When in

actually most millionaires &
billionaires never make it through
school. The only thing that makes them
different from the kids who stays in
school is determination. Most people
with an education or degree usually
gives up on trying. I mean they get
comfortable. They focus their life on
becoming that doctor, lawyer or
whatever and spend the rest of they're
life trying to become successful at their
career in working for others. What if
they receive they're degree and still
can't find a job?

90% of the working class gives up
on trying. They create a routine.
They're life becomes systematic. They
wait until they find a job "which could
be years". They never take the time to
learn anything else. A person with no
education has to use their brain a lot
more. They know that they're not

qualified for certain jobs so they create jobs or create ideals on how to make money. Not all ways of making money are successful, but something is better than nothing.

Today we live in a world of social acceptance so we try so hard to keep up with the Jones' when in fact we don't even know how the Jones' make their money or at least how they invest their money. If you ask any wealthy person what's the key to being wealthy, they'll reply "assets". 80% of the Population knows about "assets". 50% knows what's "assets" are, and only 25% actually owns any assets at all. An "asset" is just something that you own that benefits you from time to time. (Something that puts money into your pockets). The key is the more assets you have the more money you'll have coming in.

I remember a time when I didn't' have any assets at all. I use to wonder why do I make a lot of money, but I'm always broke? Just like people with jobs. It seems like every time you ask a person with a job to borrow some money they are always broke until next pay day. An individual with no income seems to always come up with money. When I was around 3 or 4 years of age my father use to have my brother, sister and I collecting recyclables such as cans, plastics, and newspapers. That was the worse thing that I thought could happen to me. Only 3 years old; and already a victim of child labor! We had to recycle just for our allowance. Some parents just give their kids allowance which leads the kids to believe that money grows on trees or at least if you beg long or hard enough you will receive the things that you desire. The only thing wrong with that is when the child gets older they realize that you don't get everything that you want just by asking. By my father making us collect cans ect. He instilled a sense that you have to work hard for the things that you want.

Even though I knew that I had to work in order to have a cash flow. I didn't know what to do with the money once I made it. Even though we get older we still have childish wants. We have an infatuation with more elaborate toys such as cars, jewelry, boats, houses, ect. We choose to buy things before we can actually afford them. What people should be doing first is building up their assets.

Have you ever filled out an application and gotten to the page that asks you to list any assets that you own? 85% marks "no" in that column.

100% of the wealthy marks "yes". And the reason that they are wealthy is because of the fact that they can mark "yes" under assets. But would that make you wealthy? Probably not, but it will put you on the path to wealth. The more assets that you have the wealthier you'll become.

The main things that the wealthy invest in are stocks, bonds, and real estate. Things that poor people invest in are cars, houses, clothes, jewelry, ect. Everything that a poor person invests in loses value or puts them in financial debt at purchase. When a person buys a house they're so happy like it's the greatest achievement in the world, but do that home buyer realize that they just put themselves in debt for the next 30 years or more? Or what about a person who leases a car? After you spend all your money on your car payments you

have to give the car back. How about
that house? You feel you have a good
job, but what if you lose your job?
How do you maintain that house? That
house that you thought was an asset
quickly becomes a liability. It comes
from a lack of understanding or should
I say everyone knows too much. Have
you ever met a person who knows
everything? But understands nothing?
It dates back to the Bible. Adam & Eve
knew that God didn't want them to eat
from the fruit from the tree of life, but
they didn't understand why they
couldn't eat from the tree. Most people
know a lot about everything. Like the
saying "A Jack of all trades, A Master
of none". That's just another way of
saying that a person knows alot, but
understands nothing. The difference
between wealthy people is that they
understand what it is they are doing.

They take the time to master whatever it is that they do which is creating a cash flow. Whether it's a minimum wage job, a good paying job, an illegal hustle, or a business. They know what to do with their money. They increase they're assets and in doing so they increase their wealth. We as humans deal with a lot of negativity or lack of encouragement that it wraps our thinking. It's like once you make a mistake or do something wrong people make it hard for us to fit back into society.

When in fact, the people who judge us are humans and also makes mistakes too. When I was in High School my brother and I were shot. My brother was shot twice in the face and twice in the shoulder. I was shot once in my right shoulder and the bullet stopped in my neck, one bullet went straight

through my left arm, when I was on the
ground I was shot in the right buttocks
which went through my stomach, and
last but not lease I was shot in the back
of my head. I was shot 8 days before
my High School Graduation. From that
day on everyone looked at me different
even though I was graduating from high
school and survived the shooting.
People started believing that I wouldn't
be successful in life. I was the type of
person who loved education but hated
discipline. When I was in school I
wanted to know everything but I didn't
want to take the time to understand it. I
would take a class just to learn the basic
fundamentals, and move on. In school
I've taken typing, band and back then
them classes were a big no, no.
Creative writing, computer graphics,
printing, and home economics. Things

that I had no use of then, but stayed with me until now.

Education was my role model. A lot of kids had no one to look up to. Especially living around poor people; and it's hard to look up to poor people, especially if you already have a cash flow. At 18 I was making $4000 a month with no job. So at that age it's hard to listen to a poor person.

So I started finding the type of people that I was interested in, in books and on television. I figured out early in life that wealthy people interested me. The only problem was that I didn't know any wealthy people that I could listen to. So once I went to prison I realized that there are a million ways to make money in this world. 85% of us only know about 4 or 5 of those ways. Business, job, credit card scams, check scams, shoplifting, robbery, extortion, selling bootleg C.D 's or D.V.D's, the list go's on and on. The key thing is not how you make your money its how you invest your money. Just like the saying time is valuable, and time is money. So if you understand that, then why not put your money to work? The same way you put yourself to work. You already understand that the harder you work the more money you make and the more money you make is the more money your money should make. Instead the more we make the more money we tend to lose. A lot of people feel as if one day they'll pick up the right book, watch the right infomercial, win the lotto, or even meet the right person and become rich. In actually only a small percentage of the world become rich that way, probably only 15% of the world. What people don't understand is that they have already

won the lotto; you have already met
that person that will make you wealthy.
That person is you. You are that special
something. You have to take risks. You
have to educate yourself on the flow of
money. You have to find out what
assets best suits you. And until you
stop looking around and start looking
inside yourself you'll never achieve
financial freedom. Wealth is not living
with a lot of money being able to buy
whatever it is you want and then dying
with nothing. No. That's the definition
of being rich. The definition of wealthy
is living your life with all those things
and then dying and passing everything
down to your kids. Then when they die
they pass everything on to your
grandkids & great grandkids and so
forth. The only thing most poor people
can pass when they die is a last name.

Who do people blame for being poor? The government... So they run down to the Department of Social Services to receive assistance. If people knew anything about finances they would instead run down to other financial insitutions. Insitutions that give grants to individuals or family's who own businesses. The average person doesn't know that it only cost about $200 to start a business, and in some places it free. General Relief pays you more than that. Instead the government sends you to programs to educate you on how to find a job in a society that they created. They don't want you to start your own business because they want you to become employees instead of employers.

For some reason it seems as if I could never get a job. It's like once you make a mistake people think that you are irresponsible. So how can you ever get a good job when people think that you are irresponsible and you have no work history? I use to think that if someone would just give me a chance and not judge me based on my past. I would be their hardest worker ever. When I was in prison I use to make 8 cents an hour and use to have to bust my ass doing hard slave labor in the desert. So I knew that if I could ever get an easy job paying at least minimum wage I would easily become the best employee. It eventually comes to a point when you say... Well hell, who cares who trust in me, I'm going to trust in myself. If you trust in yourself you'll never see yourself as a failure. And if no one ever seen you as a failure you would keep trying and wouldn't give up until something worked. But we all have too much pride. Due to the fact that you know others will see you as a failure you don't try as much or at all. Just think if Alexander Bell would have listen to all of the people who called him a failure. Even the Wright Brothers; just think about how many times they failed... Now think of how many times you've failed at trying to accomplish your goals. Probably not too many. Most people don't take risk. Most of the time the people who tell you, you won't make it, won't make it themselves.

I use to tell everyone that I was going to negotiate a 100 million dollar deal for my film & music company Big Break Entertainment. No one took me seriously. They actually thought that someone was going to walk up to me with a bunch of duffel bags full of $100 dollar bills. People thought that... because they failed to understand how money flows. See, I understand how money flows. I wasn't sitting around waiting for someone to bring me some duffel bag filled with money. "Although I wouldn't have mind seeing that". I understood that if I were going to obtain that amount of money it would have to be electronically.

I had to educate myself. I had to figure out what was worth that amount of money? And once I received that amount of money I had to make sure that I could maintain it. And not lose it all. Just because a person has a lot of money doesn't mean they can keep it. You see rich people lose riches everyday. (Entertainers with millions who file bankruptcy). That's because they don't understand money. If you spend money it disappears. So if you spend money and have no money coming in your money will disappear.

In other words if you get 10 million dollars and buy a 5 million dollar house, a few high-end cars you've already put yourself into financial debt you're just waiting for your debt to catch up to you. A person who understands the flow of money would take that same 10 million dollars and invest in as many assets as possible and live off the interest. Then let their love one's live off the interest for years to come. A lot of people feel as if they know exactly what to do; all they need is a little money or the right opportunity to get started. Just think… What if you did get that money you needed and you did start making money. Then what would you do? Spend it. You'll spend it on cars, houses, jewelry, and clothes whatever. You'll do that because you'll be considered rich, but we all know that when you die you can't take anything with you. So why not be able to pass it on to your love ones? A lot of people feel as if life insurance, houses retirement funds ect. will take care of their families once they pass away. They never know about the difficult time that their families go through to even receive a dime if in fact anything.

I use to sit and wonder why I wasn't wealthy. And then I realized that's it because my parents weren't wealthy. So wealth wasn't passed or inherited. It wasn't until I had my own kids did I realize that I had no plan for my kids future just as my parents had no plan for mines. It seems as if one year I would be partying, traveling and having fun and the next year I would be struggling. I use to listen to a lot of rich & wealthy people do interviews. They gave me hope when I would hear that half of them were at a point in their life

when they had no money and where
homeless. I use to think that I must be
on the right track because I'm broke
and homeless.

I know some of you have been there.
To much pride to go to a homeless
shelter so you buy a car to live in.
Renting a motel room for an hour just
to take a shower. More poor &
successful people have been down that
road than you can imagine. Like I
mention before there are a million ways
to create a cash flow, but remember the
only way to become wealthy is by
accumulating as many assets as
possible. Some people become wealthy
through stocks, bonds, real estate, or
some other type of investment. Some
people say they would like to help
others. Wouldn't it make sense to make
more money so that you could help
more people? Some people think that

it's too hard or too complicated. Just
remember the same way schools
produce doctors, lawyers, act. They
also produce people who can help you
manage your money. Such as Brokers,
Property Managers, C.P.A's ect.
Everything and everybody who can
help you achieve your goals. Many of
times 60% of the people around you
won't help you accomplish your goals.
And 35% of them will actually pull
you further away from your goal.
Imagine if you collect cans for 1 year
and at the end of the year you had
$1000 dollars. You take that $1000 and
buy some type of bond or C.D. Now
collect cans for one more year and at
the end of that year you'll have the
$1000 dollars that you just made, plus
the $1000 that you put into the bond or
C.D. plus the interest. Just imagine if
you kept doing that for years and years.

You'll have more bonds and more money coming in. That's what the wealthy do. They make more and more money using the least amount of labor and put it into bonds and let the interest pay for their lifestyle. It's like living for free. Or should I say financially free.

I think back to all of the people I told that I was going to be successful and they told me to get a job. People don't want to help you achieve your goal, mainly because there's a goal inside them that they haven't yet achieved. I think what got me through it all, was all of the negativity. What people don't understand is that negativity has no place in a positive world. So the more negative reactions I received from my so called friends and family was the more positive people God put into my path. I wanted to change, so I changed. I basically had to recreate myself. Deep down inside no matter how many people thought that I was a failure, I knew different. I believed in myself. When people would tell me I couldn't! I would tell myself that I could. When people told me that I would fail with Big Break Entertainment...I didn't. When people didn't think that I would write a book... I did. When people said that I would be broke my whole life...I'm not. The reason why is because I never believed them. I always believed in myself.

I remember when I got out of prison. I didn't want to do anything, not because I was lazy, but because I was on parole and I knew that I had to get off of parole if I truly wanted o live my life. People looked at me everyday like I was a bum. I use to think to myself, (that I'm just sitting around making a plan. I got my goals already I just need to create a plan to reach them). See a lot of people have a goal and no plan or a plan and with no goal. Many people know exactly what they want in life, but just don't know how to achieve it. A lot of people know how to make money but they continue to make money until they die. Some people know that they make enough money but won't buy a car, house or even invest because they feel as if it's too risky so they stay within they're comfort zone and get comfortable with their job. Remember your brain is like a battery the longer you let it sit up the longer it takes to recharge. The more that you use your brain the better you get at controlling it. Some people want to change but always complain about how they don't know how. They don't realize that in order to change yourself you must first change everything around you. You must change your way of thinking, your friends, clothes, even the places you go.

Some people don't want to stop doing the things that they need to in order to change. I know people with gambling problems. They make me upset because they comeback mad because they lost. They upset me the most because the money that they throw away is money that they could have invested. It's strange that a person would take a risk at losing money & not take a risk at gaining a guaranteed profit. Mainly because of the lack of financial education. People do not understand how money flows. Have you ever met a person who thinks he/she knows everything and tries to do everything their self instead of seeking professional help? Try to avoid people like that because they will pull you further from your goal. Like I once mentioned before. There are qualified individuals who will help you grow your money. If they charge a little find a way to fit them into your budget, because it will be well worth it.

When I was child I use to believe that only black people were poor, mainly because I am black and all I knew were black people growing up. But as I got older I started to realize that poor comes in all colors. Everybody is living in the shadows of the rich & wealthy wanting to live like them, but are afraid to take the risk like them.

That's like making a wish. When you make a wish your brain shuts down and stop trying to figure things out, but when you have dreams it's like thinking & visualizing the most beautiful & perfect place or thing that your mind can imagine. In some cases, the worst

things your mind can imagine. If
everyday or every night you dream that
you are a movie star sooner or later you
will attempt to follow your dreams and
become a movie star. Or imagine if
you were having nightmares, I'm pretty
sure you'll never stop trying to find out
what's the cause of your nightmares.
Would you not go to doctors or a
specialist? So why not go to the same
lengths to figure out your dreams when
it's a good and positive one? One time
I went down to the Department of
Social Services to apply for General
Relief. First of all the lines were to
long and the customer service was
terrible. Anyway they denied me. My
point being, that when you go down to
institutions like that they talk to you
like you're lazy and don't know any
better. When in actuality a lot of
people are just down on there luck at

the time and just needs a little help. They try to tell you that a person can't live off of $221 dollars and that you are lazy and don't want to get a job. If the government knows that it's not enough then why don't they raise it up? They won't raise it because they want you to stay in the lowest social status possible.

So why don't the government take that same time and effort to get everyone a business license? And educate everyone how to receive a grant? And if they teach us that they might as well teach us how to invest our money also. The reason they don't is because they don't want you to be financially free. Most people who are poor choose to be poor. Remember everybody have choices, whether you make the right or wrong ones is also your choice. If you choose to stop being broke you will. Once you choose to change you will set your mind to it and never stop until you change. Think about it; if you don't believe in yourself then who else will? Always remember if you can look the part, then you can play the part.

A long time along I didn't understand how important my name was. Actually I didn't even like my name. I disliked my name so much that I had a nick name that I use to go by. We never take the time to think of how important or names are. Take the time right now and think about why a persons name is so important? Exactly; your name is the key to your fortune. Based on your name along you can get money, cars, houses, food anything you want. Just think just based on who you are you can get anything. Look at O.J he beat his case based on his name. Your name can be very powerful if you learn how to build and harness that power. Take Michael Jackson for instance his name is very powerful. He can go anywhere in the world and be recognized. If he was on the phone and ordered something he will get the best service based on his name alone. Think about how powerful your name is. There was a time when I felt as if I was the man on the block making so much money because everybody knew who I was. One day I went to a car lot and tried to get a car. They ran my credit (which is my name) they told me that my name wasn't good enough. They told me that I had to go and find someone whose name was alittle more established than mines. They basically were telling that no matter how much money I made, if I didn't' invest and get some type of ownership in my life;

then my name wouldn't ever be worth anything.

How many people have been told the same thing in life? That your name just isn't good enough. I'm pretty sure at least half of ya'll have experienced this. When we're young we take our names for granted just think about identity theft, people can commit a crime and use you name, and you'll go to jail. So always protect your name and build the power in your name. Invest in things, start a business, build your credit. Your name is your wealth. That's all wealth is; How many years after your death will your name live on and be profitable. Think about Elvis, Tupac, Walt Disney or even the Hilton's those names are names that will bring wealth for there families for generation after generation.

Here are a few things that I use to think of to motivate me though tuff times. These are also some of the things that I use to tell anyone who would come to me for advice.

- 4 rubber wheels beat 2 rubber heels. (Any car is better than walking).
- Put your pride aside.
- The more people that you help the more people that will help you.
- Money is not the root to all evil. (That's just a saying that someone started to psychologically keep us from wanting to understand the flow of money).
- Protect your credit. Many people do not know about credit but believe me one day you'll need it so work at building it.
- If you have negative people or things around you get rid of them

because negative and positive
things do not mix.

- Put other people to work. If you
can hire someone to help you
make money do it. Even the
wealthy have employees in some
form or fashion.

So remember, No matter what you do
Don't panic. There will always be a
second chance. You'll always have
another opportunity. Unless you're
dead. Then you get no more chances.
You're game is over. Well I hope that
you enjoyed some of the things that
were on my mind and I hope that they
were helpful. Some what ever you do
keep a smile on your face and a song in
your heart.

One Flaw In Women

By the time the Lord made women, He
was into his sixth day of working
overtime. An angel appeared and said,
"Why are you spending so much time
on this one?" The Lord answered,
"Have you seen my spec sheet on her?"
She has to be completely washable, but
not plastic. Have over 200 moveable
parts, all replaceable and able to run on
diet coke and leftovers. Have a lap that
can hold four children at one time.
Have a kiss that can cure anything from
a scraped knee to a broken heart, and
she will do everything with only two
hands.

The angel was astounded at the requirements. "Only two hands? No way! And that's just on the standard model. That's too much work for on day. Wait until tomorrow to finish." "I won't." the Lord protested. "I am so close to finishing this creation that is so close to my heart. She already heals herself when she is sick, and can work 18 hours a day." The angel moved closer and touched the woman. "But you have made her so soft, Lord." "She is soft" the Lord agreed. "But I have also made her tough. You have no idea what she can endure or accomplish." "Will she be able to think?" asked the angel. The Lord replied, "Not only will she be able to think, she will be able to reason and negotiate." The angel noticed something and reaching out, touched the woman's cheek. "Oops, it looks like you have a leak in this

model. I corrected. "That's a tear."
"What's it for?" the angel asked. The
Lord said, "The tear is her way of
expressing her joy, her sorrow, her
pain, her disappointment, her love, her
loneliness, her grief, and her pride."
The angel was impressed. "You are a
genius, Lord. You thought of
everything! Women are truly amazing;
and she is!"

Women have strengths that amaze
men. They bear the hardships and they
carry the burdens, but they hold
happiness, love, and joy. They smile
when they want to scream, They sing
when they want to cry. They cry when
they are happy, and laugh when they
are nervous. They fight for what they
believe in. They stand up for justice.
They don't take "no" for an answer
when they believe there is a better
solution. They go without so their

family can have. They go to the doctor with a frightened. They love unconditionally. They cry when their children excel, and cheer when their friends get awards. They are happy when they hear about a birth or a wedding. Their hearts break when a friend dies. They grieve at the loss of a family member, yet they are strong when they think there is no strength left. They know that a hug and a kiss can heal a broken heart. Women come in all shapes, sizes, and colors. They'll drive, fly, walk, run, or e-mail you to show how much they care about you. The heart of a woman is what makes the world keep turning. They bring joy, hope, and love. They have compassions and ideals. They give moral support to their family and friends. Women have vital things to say and everything to give.

However, if there is **one** flaw in women…
It is that they sometimes forget their worth.

Dedicated to
Cleavotta Algeria Piggie

Special Thanks:

The H.E.L.P Foundation
helpingeveryonelovepeole@yahoo.com

A List Clothing Company
alistclothingcompany@yahoo.com

D.A.M Film Productions

damfilmproductions@yahoo.com

Big Break Entertainment
labigbreakentertainment@yahoo.com

Poem One Flaw In Women comes from Lily
of the Valley Church. Courtesy of Pastor
James Shaw.

Who needs a Mayor who lies, cheats, and takes vacations all year when people in Los Angeles are losing their homes, jobs, families, and freedom. No more Villaraigosa!!! We need a real Mayor not someone who looks good being the Mayor.

The H.E.L.P. Foundation, Inc. is a 501 (c)(3) non-profit organization based in Long Beach Ca., is submitting this letter of intent to determine your interest in providing funding for our program which aspires to be a resource to children by nurturing and supporting them educationally, physically and economically. Our mission is to be an organization that produces social changes in all children of all ethnicities and ages. We want to bring quality of life to the children of this country by offering them encouragement and resources to develop in all areas of their life.

In our research of possible funding sources, we discovered that your foundation also has a strong interest in human services, community development and children. Our proposed project will help you achieve your own goals for humanity.

Recognizing the needs that exist in United States, the organization has developed plans to assist children in their educational pursuits and setting goals for their lives, but also in gang reforms and providing scholarship to those individuals looking to pursue higher eduction.

In 2008, The H.E.L.P. Foundation,Inc hopes to:

- Secure building, computers and all necessary items to start the programs so that the organization can accommodate up to 25 children.
- Build relationships with individuals to bring on as staff members in order to be a positive influence on all children in the program.

We look forward to further discussions about our program and this letter of intent. If you have any questions about The H.E.L.P Foundation,Inc., please do not hesitate to contact me at helpingeveryonelovepeople@yahoo.com or www.helpingeveryonelovepeople.org

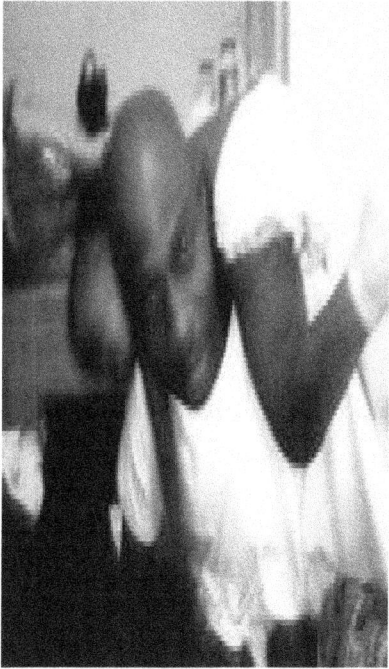

Big Break Entertainment

labigbreakentertainment@yahoo.com

Alist Clothing Company

Clothes For, The Elite.

alistclotingcompanycompany@yahoo.com

D.A.M
Film,
Productions

damfilmproductions@yahoo.com

www.ingramcontent.com/pod-product-compliance
Lightning Source LLC
Chambersburg PA
CBHW020527030426
42337CB00011B/567